BIG BROTHER BLUES

BIG
BROTHER
BLUES

THE EDITORIAL CARTOONS
OF BEN SARGENT

★

Although the concept of this book was inspired by the works of George Orwell, it is not authorized by him or his Estate. It should not be confused with the novel *1984* and is not associated with the motion picture *1984* or any remake.

Ben Sargent's cartoons are syndicated by United Features Syndicate.

Texas Monthly Press
P.O. Box 1569
Austin, Texas 78767

A   B   C   D   E   F   G   H

Library of Congress Cataloging in Publication Data

Sargent, Ben, 1948–
  Big brother blues.

  1. United States—Politics and government—1981-
Caricatures and cartoons.   2. American wit and humor,
Pictorial.   I. Title.
F876.S27   1984   973.92   84-2665
ISBN 0-932012-94-9

For Diane . . .

. . . and for Elizabeth

Pssst . . . hey, comrade!

That's right, over here! Yeah, it's me . . . Big Brother!

Hey, don't look so nervous. . . .
I'm not really such a bad guy, if
you get to know me. . . . It
even gets a little lonesome,
y'know, being Big Brother . . .

Ever try to make friends when people think you're omnipresent? Ever try to get dates when everybody thinks you're all-powerful? Hah?

I'm telling you, it's tough. . . . Everybody blames me for all this 1984 stuff . . . Newspeak! Thoughtcrime! And Doublethink! You think I *invented* Doublethink? Heck, no!

Doublethink's been around at least since the time of Little Brother and his proposition that Bumbling Is Competence. . . . Then along came Older Brother, with his idea that Backward Is Forward. . . . Hey, whose Doublethink d'ya buy?

9

12

BEN SARGENT...
©1980 The Austin American-Statesman...

15

21

BEN SARGENT...
©1980 The Austin American-Statesman...

FRIENDS, YOU'RE GONNA HEAR A LOTTA BALONEY IN THIS CAMPAIGN ABOUT EXPERIENCE!

REAGAN HEADQUARTERS

THEY SAY I'M INEXPERIENCED IN FOREIGN AFFAIRS! INEXPERIENCED? WHAT ABOUT "INTERNATIONAL SQUADRON"? WHAT ABOUT "HONG KONG"?

THEY THINK I HAVEN'T HAD EXPERIENCE WITH NATIONAL DEFENSE? DIDN'T THEY SEE "PRISONER OF WAR"? "HELLCATS OF THE NAVY"?

BEN SARGENT...
© 1980 The Austin American-Statesman...

"BEDTIME FOR BONZO"! "BONZO GOES TO COLLEGE"! WHAT ABOUT THAT? HAH?

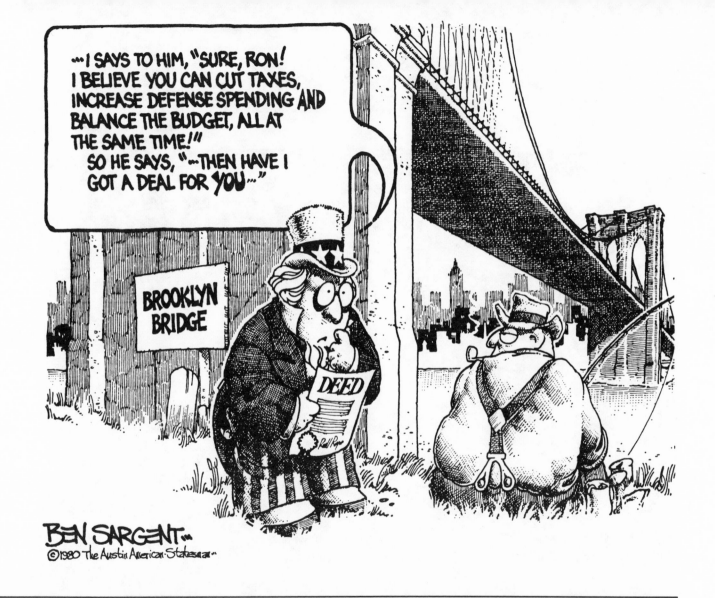

THE 1980 CAMPAIGN ACADEMY AWARDS!

SAMMY

TOO CLOSE TO CALL

★MOST INCREDIBLE FANTASY... JOHN ANDERSON

★BEST DISASTER EPIC- JIMMY CARTER IN "THE HERBERT HOOVER STORY"

★MOST BUNGLED SCENARIO-WRITING... THE POLLSTERS

TIME FOR A NEW BEGINNING

★BEST ACTOR IN A LEADING ROLE- (ONLY ONE NOMINATED)

★WORST RE-MAKE OF A PERFORMANCE THAT WAS TERRIBLE THE FIRST TIME... THE MORAL RIGHT IN "JOE McCARTHY, ALL-AMERICAN"

★LEAST SNAPPY SLOGAN- LIBERTARIAN PARTY

★BEST CHILD IN A POLICY-MAKING ROLE- AMY CARTER

BEN SARGENT- ©1980 The Austin American-Statesman

PLUTOCRACY

IS PROSPERITY

Listen . . . Doublethink'd never seen the likes of Older Brother. . . . Take his ideas about economics. . . . He proposed to spend more, take in less, balance the two, make the rich richer and leave everybody happier . . . all at the same time! Why, the old-fashioned Doublethink I was familiar with never tried to handle more than two contradictions at one time. . . . Oh, I knew a *master* had arrived . . .

FOLK REMEDIES...

A SWEET POTATO IN YOUR LEFT HIP POCKET WILL CURE ARTHRITIS.

GARLIC WORN AROUND THE NECK IN A DIRTY SOCK WILL PREVENT A COLD.

TURNING A SOMERSAULT WHEN THE FIRST WHIPPOORWILL CALLS WILL PREVENT BACKACHE.

A MASSIVE TAX CUT WILL CURE INFLATION.

OH, DON'T BE RIDICULOUS!

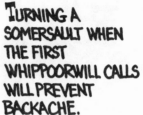

BEN SARGENT...
©1981 The Austin American-Statesman/2

35

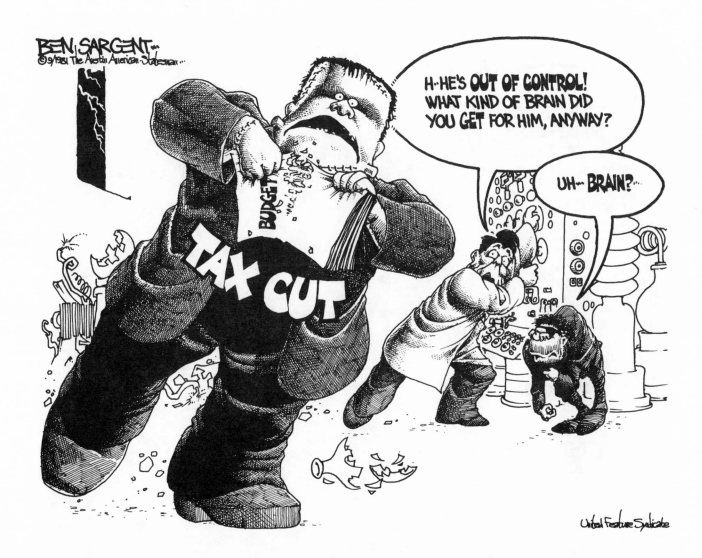

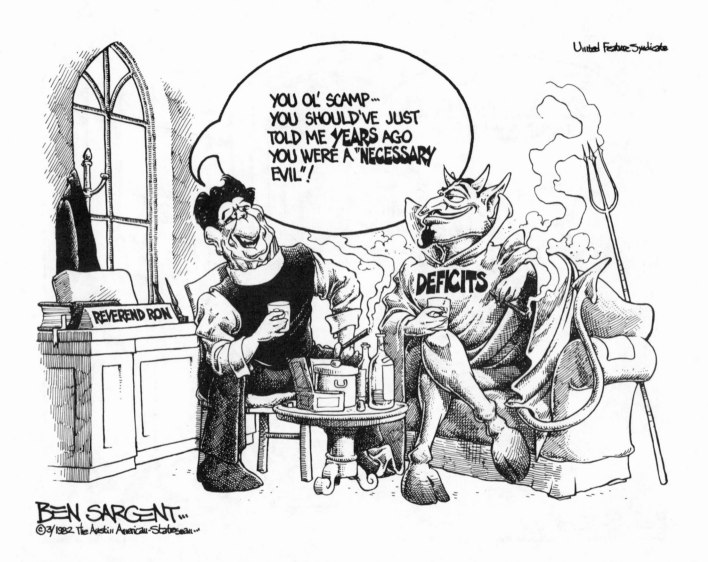

THE LITTLE TOY DOG IS
    COVERED WITH DUST,
BUT STURDY AND STAUNCH
    IT STANDS;
AND THE LITTLE TOY SOLDIER
    IS RED WITH RUST,
AND HIS MUSKET MOLDS
    IN HIS HANDS;
TIME WAS WHEN THE LITTLE
    TOY DOG WAS NEW,
AND THE SOLDIER WAS
    PASSING FAIR;
AND THAT WAS THE TIME WHEN
    OUR LITTLE BOY BLUE
KISSED THEM AND
    PUT THEM THERE.

--- Eugene Field

BEN SARGENT...
© 11/1982 the Austin American-Statesman...

WHITE HOUSE
ATTIC

1984
BALANCED
BUDGET

United Feature Syndicate

48

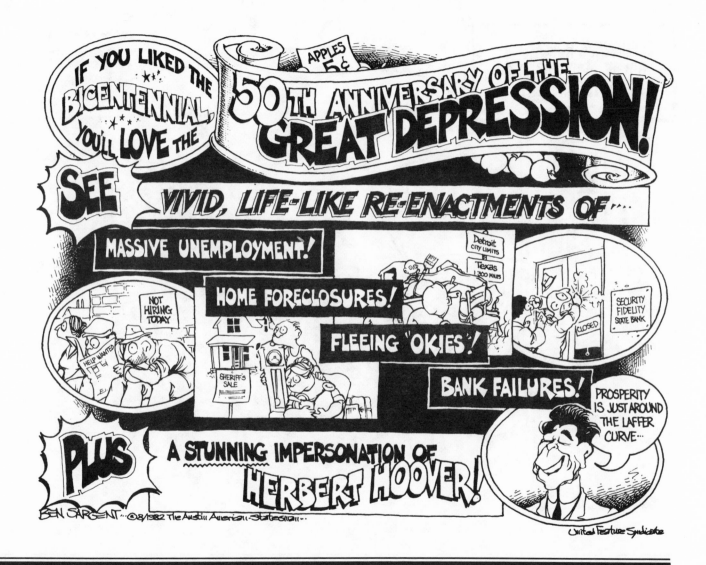

BEN SARGENT..
©9/1982 The Austin American-Statesman

United Feature Syndicate

Old Mother Hubbard
went to the cupboard,
She needed food but
couldn't buy it...

But when she
got there
The cupboard
was bare...
We call it the
"Ron Reagan Diet"...

SORRY!
—Ron

FOOD STAMPS

BREAD LINE ~ 1930

'BREAD' LINE ~ 1980

BEN SARGENT...
© 1980 The Austin American-Statesman
United Feature Syndicate...

You can help feed a hungry millionaire. Or you can turn the page.

SURE, LITTLE MORTON PELF WON'T GO TO BED COLD OR HUNGRY TONIGHT --- AS A HIGH-LEVEL CORPORATE EXECUTIVE, HIS ANNUAL CAPITAL GAINS ALONE DWARF WHAT YOU'LL MAKE IN A LIFETIME --- BUT MORT HAS A NEED FOR MORE AND MORE DOUGH THAT ONLY THE REALLY RICH CAN UNDERSTAND.

Here's how you can help!

YOUR VOTE FOR RONALD REAGAN CAN MEAN A TAX-CUT BONANZA FOR RICH PEOPLE LIKE LITTLE MORT --- AND HE'LL NEVER HAVE TO LUST AFTER LUCRE AGAIN!

Save the Wealthy, Inc

BEN SARGENT
© 1980 The Austin American-Statesman

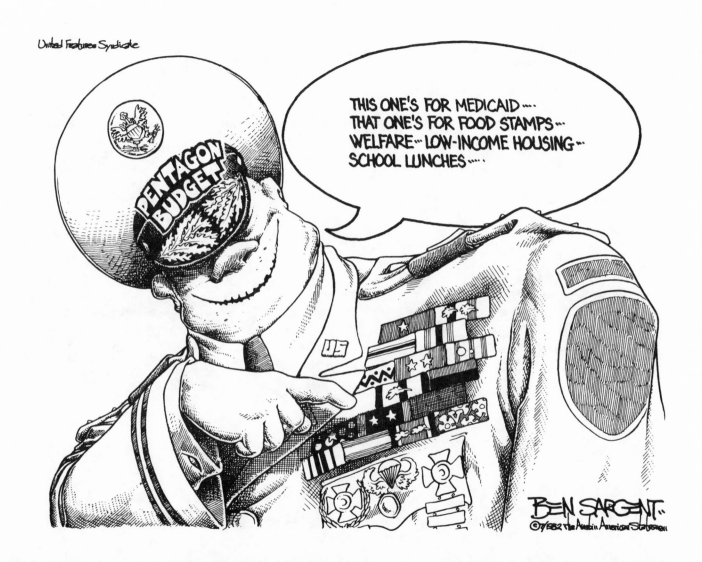

WELFARE CADILLAC. WARFARE CADILLACS.

Older Brother's Backward-Is-Forward economics waded into the environment with both hands grabbing, since exploitative economics are lost without a world to exploit. . . . The environment nearly proved a match for Older Brother and his crew, though, in spite of their energy.

68

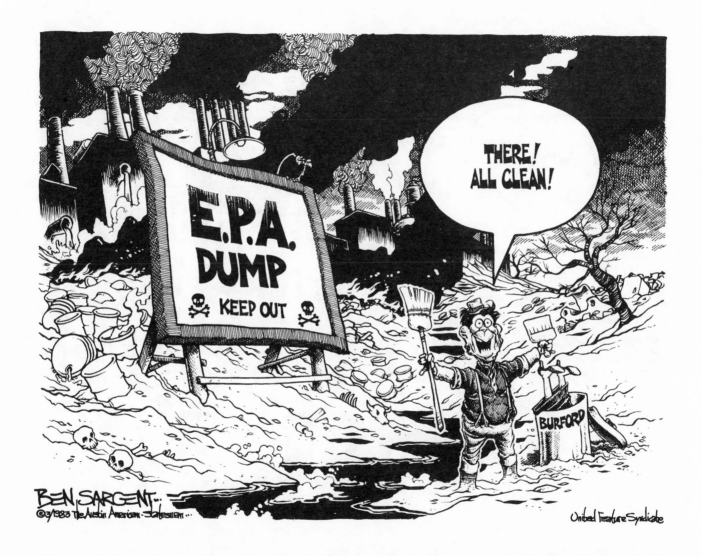

Older Brother's crew ... now there's a piece of work! His environmental elves weren't the only brotherlings up to mischief. ... No, Older Brother had a talent for picking subordinates who ranged from the eccentric to the simply ignorant. ... Now, I know there was a general outbreak of strangeness and aggressive ignorance going on at the time, but still ...

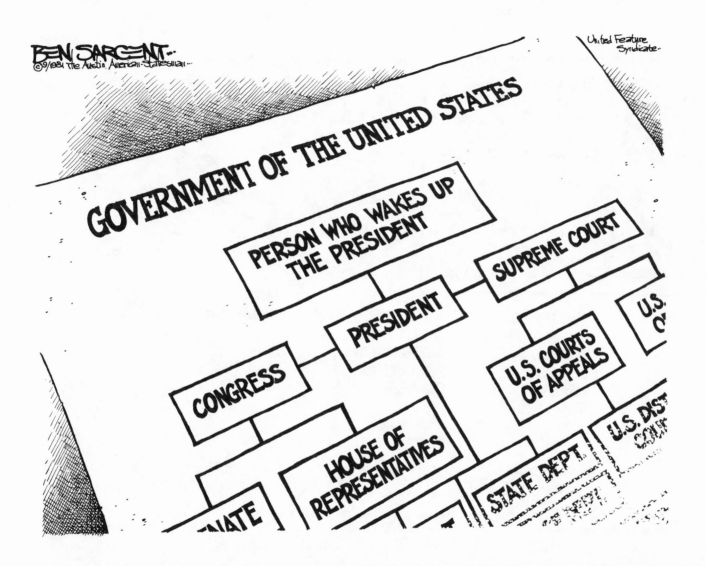

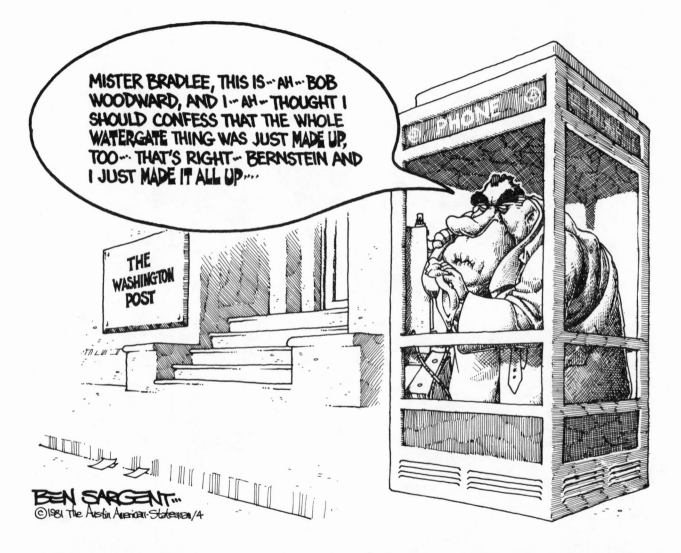

THE UNITED STATES HAS THE MOST SOPHISTICATED AND PERVASIVE INTELLIGENCE NETWORK IN THE WORLD....

DAY AND NIGHT, ALL AROUND THE GLOBE, THE CIA, THE DEFENSE INTELLIGENCE AGENCY, THE FBI, MILITARY INTELLIGENCE AND THE NATIONAL SECURITY AGENCY ARE HARD AT WORK....

MOUNTAINS OF RAW DATA POUR IN, NOT JUST FROM SECRET AGENTS, BUT FROM FOREIGN BROADCASTS, FOREIGN PUBLICATIONS, DIPLOMATS AND OTHER OBSERVERS....

WE'VE GOT ELECTRONIC EAVESDROPPING ON PLANES, SHIPS AND THE GROUND THAT CAN HEAR 'EM SNEEZE ON A SOVIET SUB.... WE'VE GOT AIR AND SPACE RECONNAISSANCE THAT CAN READ THE SERIAL NUMBER ON A RUSSIAN RIFLE....

BEN SARGENT

ALL THIS DATA IS EVALUATED FOR SOURCE RELIABILITY AND INFORMATION ACCURACY, COMPLEX INFORMATION IS COMPUTER ANALYZED, CATALOGUED AND STORED FOR RETRIEVAL....

©1982 The Austin American-Statesman

THEN IT'S ALL PUT AT THE FINGERTIPS OF TH' PRESIDENT, RIGHT?

OH GOSH NO.... HE HAS HIS OWN SOURCES....

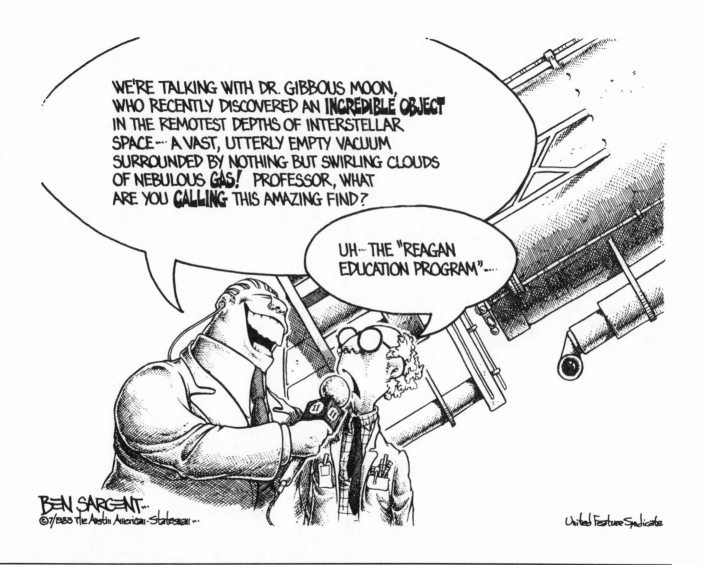

Civil liberties . . . now we're back on my home turf, right? I mean, what does the idea "1984" suggest, if not state snoopery, pathological secrecy, squashing people's rights . . . hey? Well, I'm afraid Older Brother beats me out on this one, too . . . and a neat piece of Doublethink it is, what with Older Brother billing himself as the champion of individual freedom. . . .

WE'VE TRIED T' CLEAR 'EM OUT, WARDEN-- BUT THEY'RE STILL DOWN THERE---

KILL 'EM! SLAUGHTER 'EM ALL!

LET US AT 'EM!

BURN 'EM! PULL TH' SWITCH!

LEMME TRY---

LISTEN UP, YOU SAVAGES! TAKE YOUR BLOOD LUST SOMEWHERE ELSE! IF WE EXECUTE ANYBODY, IT'LL BE ACCORDING TO TH' LAW, NOT TO SATE A LYNCH MOB!!

WE STILL HAVE LAWS IN THIS COUNTRY, YOU KNOW! WE STILL HAVE A CONSTITUTION!!

NOBODY GETS EXECUTED AROUND HERE UNTIL THE SUPREME COURT- OH MY LORD---

---THAT IS THE SUPREME COURT---

GIVE 'EM TH' HOT SQUAT!!

FRY 'EM!

BEN SARGENT---
©1984 The Austin American-Statesman

United Features Syndicate

While Older Brother was pushing an early 1984 for civil liberties, he was pushing Backward Is Forward for equal rights too.... Those that weren't white and male, he gave even more to worry about....

Reasoning together, Older Brother thought, was a complicated and messy way of dealing with his brother countries. . . . Let us, says he, choose up sides instead for little wars of good against evil. . . . Briskly simple approach, I'll admit, but it seems a Doublethink way of making the world a more secure place. . . . It's a whole world of little wars, y'know, it's a hard game to leave once you're in it.

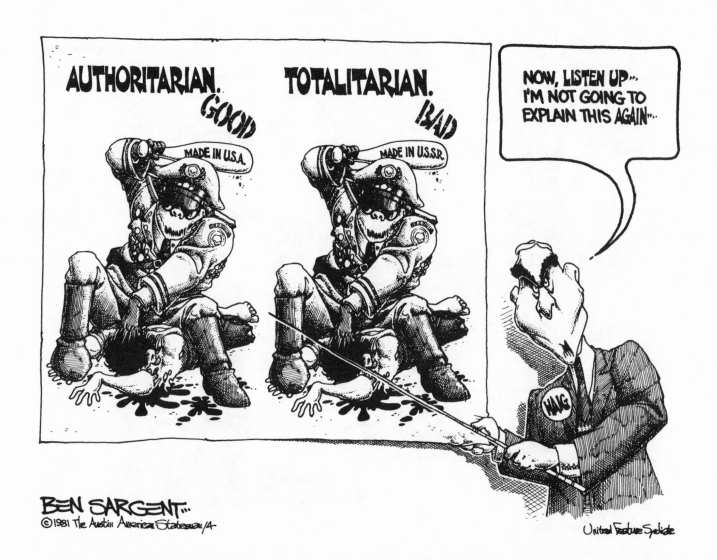

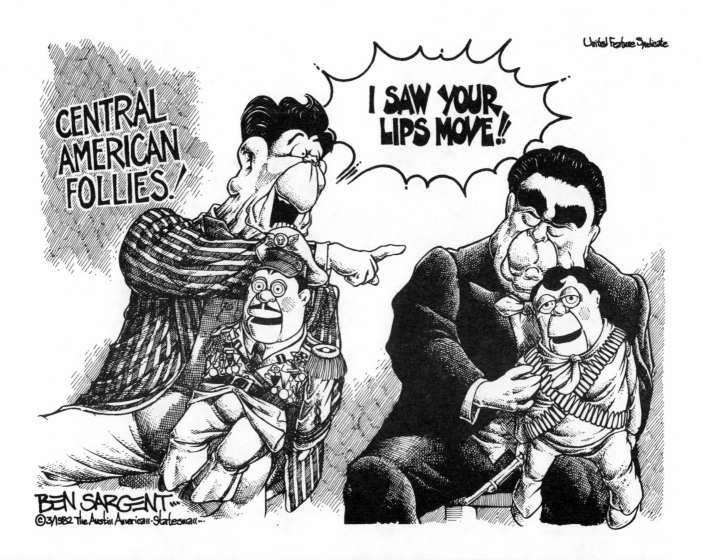

United Feature Syndicate

BEN SARGENT...
©4/1983 the Austin American-Statesman

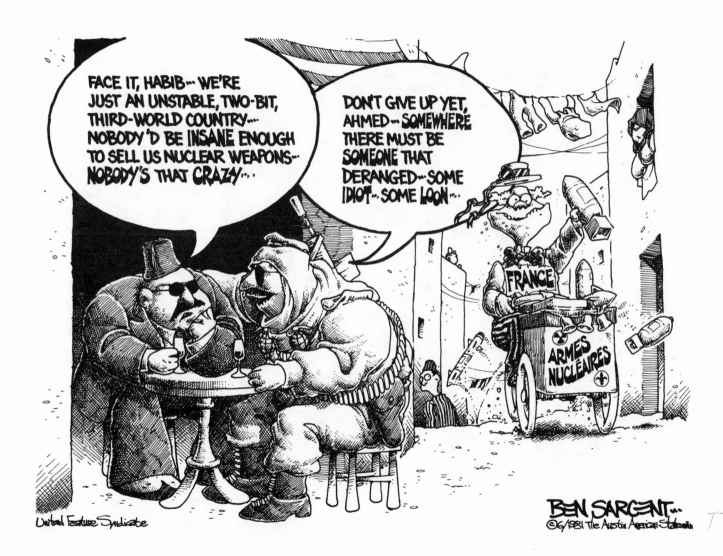

Now, of course, as adept as Older Brother was at Doublethink, I can't let you think *he* invented it any more than *I* did. . . . If anybody ought to get credit for spawning and perfecting Doublethink, it's our brothers in the Soviet Union. . . . You name it . . . War Is Peace, Freedom Is Slavery, Ignorance Is Strength . . . nobody else approaches the genuine originals for four-wheel, big-league, industrial-strength Doublethink. . . .

Watch for bold new leadership from our new party
chairman, insiders say....Unlike most in the Kremlin,
Comrade Andropov is open-minded, charming, sophisticated....
Sure, he was head of the brutal, ruthless KGB for 15
years, but if affable, urbane Comrade Yuri is the
closet liberal he seems to be, the days of
repression are ov e

r

BEN SARGENT...
©11/1982 The Austin American-Statesman

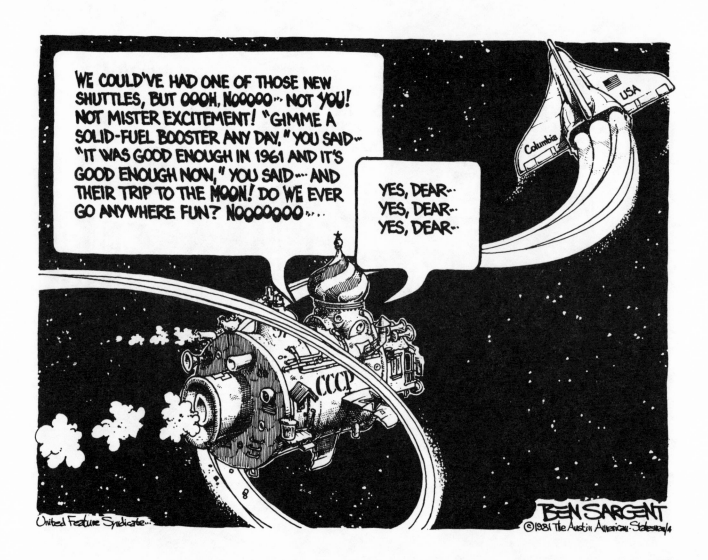

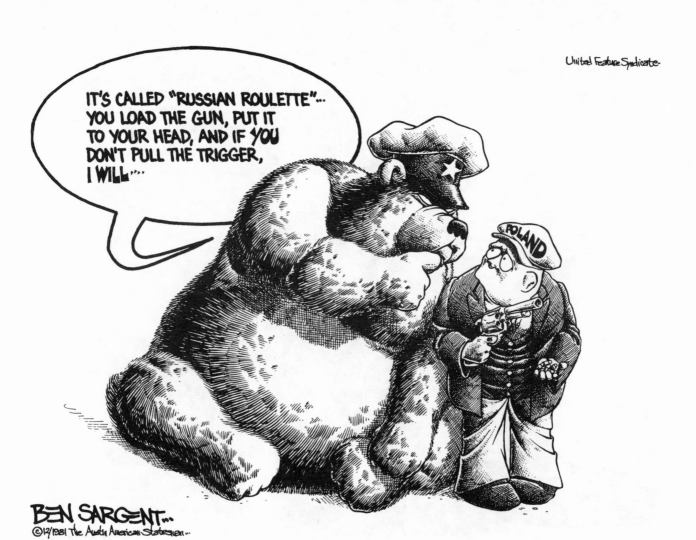

SOLIDAR...

MILITARY RULE

BEN SARGENT...
© 5/1982 The Austin American-Statesman

BEN SARGENT...
©1980 The Austin American-Statesman...

But whoever came up with Doublethink, people on both sides of the globe seem equally prone to the ultimate Doublethink, and this little rascal is to blame. . . . See? It's an atom . . . and the day a human being first split one of these and unleashed its power, the whole language was turned on its head. . . . Takes Doublethink to its breaking point to call a nuclear weapon a "weapon," or nuclear war a "war." . . . That ultimate event would take weapons, war, language, Doublethink, you, me, everything, up in its flames. . . .

GUIDE TO A NUCLEAR EXPLOSION
···FOR THOSE WHO THINK WE COULD HIDE FROM ONE····

25-MEGATON BOMB, DETONATED 3 MILES IN THE AIR.

200-MILLION-DEGREE FIREBALL, 8 MILES HIGH, VAPORIZES EVERYTHING WITHIN 6 MILES.

WITHIN 80 MILES, EXPOSED PEOPLE SUFFER FROM BURNS, BLINDNESS, FLYING DEBRIS.

WITHIN 30 MILES, HEAT WAVE INCINERATES EVERYTHING FLAMMABLE, BLAST WAVE PULVERIZES EVERYTHING ELSE.

30-MILE-HIGH CLOUD OF RADIOACTIVE DUST SPREADS RADIATION OVER THOUSANDS OF SQUARE MILES. "SURVIVORS" FACE RADIATION SICKNESS, EPIDEMICS AND CONTAMINATED AIR, SOIL, FOOD AND WATER····

BEN SARGENT···
©1982 The Austin American-Statesman···

SUICIDAL CASES.

United Feature Syndicate

BEN SARGENT..
©1982 The Austin American-Statesman..

I'LL NOT HAVE THIS COUNTRY LOCKED IN BY ANY "NUCLEAR FREEZE"... NO SIR! FIRST WE GET **EVEN-UP** WITH THE SOVIETS... **THEN** WE'LL TALK!

ALL RIGHT, GENERAL... TELL THE FOLKS WHAT WE HAVE TO DO TO MAKE OUR STRATEGIC NUCLEAR FORCE EQUAL TO RUSSIA'S ...

BEN SARGENT
© 1982 The Austin American-Statesman

WELL, SIR,... UH... SCRAP THE CRUISE-MISSILE PROGRAM, GET SOME NOISIER AND LESS-RELIABLE SUBMARINES, GET RID OF ABOUT 2,000 NUCLEAR WEAPONS, DOWNGRADE...

YEAH, BUT DID YOU HEAR THE ONE ABOUT THE RUSSIAN WITH AN ORANGE IN ONE HAND AND A BOTTLE OF VODKA IN THE OTHER? HAH?

United Feature Syndicate

148

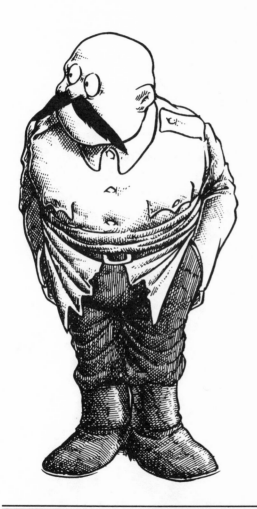

Well . . . I guess you knew when 1984 rolled in, you'd see me around, and Doublethink too. . . . I had no idea it'd be quite so *vigorous*. . . . But I think you've got the best antidote to Doublethink right at hand, and that's knowing it when you see it. . . .

You keep trusting your instincts on that account, and the 1984 you read about can't ever arrive.... And remember...

I'll be watching you. . . .